# On your First Holy Communion

*Selected by*
*Andrew Moore*

**Augsburg Books**
MINNEAPOLIS

ON YOUR FIRST HOLY COMMUNION

Copyright © 2006 Andrew Moore
Original edition published in English under the title ON YOUR FIRST
HOLY COMMUNION by Kevin Mayhew Ltd, Buxhall, England.
This edition copyright © Fortress Press 2019

All rights reserved. Except for brief quotations in critical articles or reviews,
no part of this book may be reproduced in any manner without prior
written permission from the publisher. Email copyright@augsburgfortress.org
or write to Permissions, Fortress Press, PO Box 1209, Minneapolis, MN
55440-1209.

Pages 18 and 20: Roman Missal © 1973, 1974, ICEL Inc., 1522 K Street,
NW Suite 1000, Washington DC 20005-1202 USA. Used by permission.
All other texts © Kevin Mayhew Ltd.

Scripture quotations taken from The Jerusalem Bible, published and
copyright 1966, 1967 and 1968 by DLT Ltd and Doubleday and Co Inc.
Used by permission.

Cover image: Cover art from book interior
Cover design: Alisha Lofgren

Print ISBN: 978-1-5064-5936-3

To celebrate
the First Communion of

..................................................................

At ............................................................

On ............................................................

From ..........................................................

Lord Jesus,
I like the quietness of Holy Communion—
quiet voices,
quiet feet,
quiet music.
We are quiet because we know that you are here.
Your Spirit whispers to us.
Your holiness is all around us
as you feed us with the bread and wine.
Was it like that at the Last Supper?

*Peter Dainty*

He rained down manna for their food,
and gave them bread from heaven.
Mere mortals ate the bread of angels.
He sent them abundance of food.

*Psalm 78:24, 25*

"I am the living bread which has come down from heaven," says the Lord. Anyone who eats this bread will live forever.

*John 6:51, 52 (Jerusalem Bible)*

Taste and see that the Lord is good.

*Psalm 34:8*

Jesus took the five loaves and the two fish, raised his eyes to heaven, and said the blessing over them; then he broke them and handed them to his disciples to distribute among the crowd. They all ate as much as they wanted, and when the scraps remaining were collected they filled twelve baskets.

*Luke 9:15–17 (Jerusalem Bible)*

"I am the vine and you are the branches," says the Lord. "Whoever lives in me, and I in them, will bear much fruit."

*John 15:5*

Jesus, I know I can only produce good fruit
if I'm connected to you, the true vine.
Let your life flow into me and through me
so together we can make a huge harvest.

*Susan Sayers*

This is my body, broken for you,
bringing you wholeness, making you free.
Take it and eat it, and when you do,
do it in love for me.

This is my blood, poured out for you,
bringing forgiveness, making you free.
Take it and drink it, and when you do,
do it in love for me.

Love one another; I have loved you,
and I have shown you how to be free;
serve one another, and when you do,
do it in love for me.

*Jimmy Owens and Damian Lundy*

The two disciples told their story of how
they had met Jesus on the road to Emmaus
and how they had recognized him
in the breaking of the bread.

*Luke 24:35*

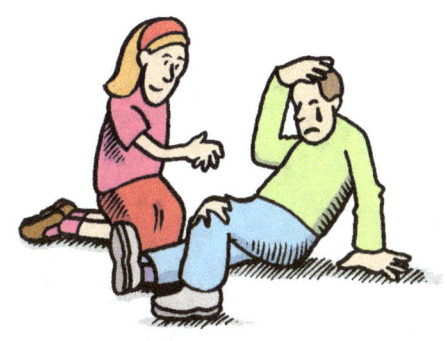

Eternal God,
your Son Jesus Christ broke bread
to feed a hungry people
and to bring new life to a broken world.
When we break bread in his name,
fill us with his life
and send us out
to share his love with others.

*Leslie J. Francis and Diane Drayson*

If "Eucharist" means "Thanksgiving,"
then, Lord, I must give you thanks for so many things:

Thank you for making me, me,
thank you for my parents and my family,
thank you for my friends and all I meet
and for this special food you give us to eat.

And if "Communion" means "being one with,"
then, Lord, I must try "to be one with" so many things:

Help me "to be one with" the beauty of creation,
help me "to be one with" people of every nation,
help me "to be one with" my true self
through this special gift of yourself.

*Andrew Moore*

Lord, you renew us at your table
with the bread of life.
May this food strengthen us in love
and help us to serve you in each other.

*Roman Missal post-Communion prayer 22B*

Loving Father, thank you for feeding us
with food for our bodies and our souls,
making us strong
so we can live good, loving lives.
Amen.

*Susan Sayers*

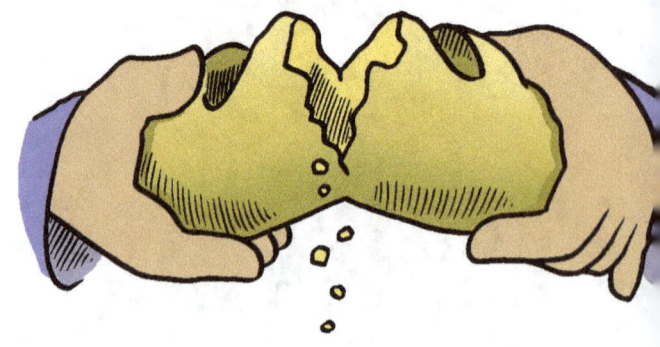

Blessed are you, Lord, God of all creation.
Through your goodness we have this bread to offer
which earth has given and human hands have made.
It will become for us the bread of life.
Blessed be God forever.

Blessed are you, Lord, God of all creation.
Through your goodness we have this wine to offer
which earth has given and human hands have made.
It will become our spiritual drink.
Blessed be God forever.

*Offering prayers from the Mass*

John the Baptist saw Jesus coming toward him and said, "Look, there is the Lamb of God who takes away the sin of the world."

*John 1:29*

Loving Father God,
I praise and thank you.
You are great and you are wonderful.
Thank you for sending Jesus
to be my friend and to help me.
Thank you for sending your Holy Spirit
to make me strong.
Thank you for forgiving my sins
and for loving me forever.

*Joan Brown*

Jesus, you died for me.
Your body is the broken bread
I share in Holy Communion.
Your spilled blood is given in the wine.

But you defeated death,
and no earthly rock could hold you down.

Because of you,
I am raised up too.
Thank you for the gift of eternal life.
Amen.

*Susan Hardwick*

Just as in our human life we need food and drink,
so in our spiritual life we need Christ to nourish
and sustain us. He feeds us with himself,
with his words, through Scripture, and with the
Sacrament of his Body and his Blood.
As we eat together the sacred bread and wine
we share with one another, so the community
is made strong as we grow personally in strength.

*Tony Castle*

The blessing-cup that we bless is a communion
with the blood of Christ, and the bread we break
is a communion with the body of Christ.
The fact that there is only one loaf means that,
though there are many of us, we form a single body
because we all have a share in this one loaf.

*1 Corinthians 10:16, 17 (Jerusalem Bible)*

Christ with me,
Christ before me,
Christ behind me,
Christ within me,
Christ beneath me,
Christ above me,
Christ at my right,
Christ at my left,
Christ in the heart of everyone who thinks of me,
Christ in the mouth of everyone who speaks to me,
Christ in every eye that sees me,
Christ in every ear that hears me.

*From St Patrick's Breastplate*

www.ingramcontent.com/pod-product-compliance
Lightning Source LLC
Chambersburg PA
CBHW052038070526
44584CB00020B/3159